1

Kangaroos *kan-ga-roos*, lived all over Australia. There are many kinds of kangaroos. This is a large kangaroo that no longer exists. Some kangaroos are very small. The First People used kangaroos for food and fur.

3

There are many types of possums in Australia. Possums live above the ground. Possums live in trees. The First People used possums for food and fur.

5

This is a large Australian lizard. It is called a goanna. It is strong and has sharp claws. Goannas can climb trees. The First People used goannas for food.

7

The emu is a bird. It is a bird which cannot fly. It lives across Australia. The First People ate the eggs of the emu. The emu was also used for food.

The emu egg is dark green. The emu would hide the egg. The egg is the same colour as the grasses. The First People would eat the eggs.

11

This is an Australian python. The python lived in the forests. The python ate small animals and eggs. The First People used pythons for food.

Ducks lived on lagoons and rivers in Australia. There were many types of ducks. The First People used ducks for food.

15

This is a numbat. The numbat eats only termites found in the soil. The numbat is only found in Western Australia. It is a very rare animal.

17

The wombat has strong claws to dig. It digs holes and sleeps below ground. It eats grasses, small plants and some roots. The First People used the wombat for food and fur.

19

Koalas lived all over Australia. The koala only eats the leaves of gum trees. The koala needs a forest of trees to live in. The First People used the koala for food and fur.

21

This large bird no longer exists. It is called Genyornis *geny-or-nis*. The Genyornis may have been used by the First People for food.

23

Word bank

kangaroo

Australia

possum

ground

goanna

lizard

difficult

python

termites

rare